Bella Saves the Farm

DIANE ODEGARD GOCKEL

ISBN: 0989631710
ISBN 13: 9780989631716

DEDICATION

To my beautiful daughter Julie, who is also my business partner and my friend, who shares my love for all little homeless and neglected pets. And to her and her husband's first baby on the way; I love you already. And, of course, to our beautiful Bella who really did save our farm.

ABOUT THE AUTHOR

Diane Odegard Gockel is a former high school teacher who has devoted much of her life to the rescue, fostering and adoption of homeless pets. She and her daughter Julie Diane Stafford co-own Creative Kids Unplugged. Diane and her husband have four grown children and live on a small farm in Sammamish, Washington called Second Chance Ranch.

The Farm Lady's oldest daughter named me Bella, which means "beautiful girl". My parents are both working border collies that live at neighboring farms. When the man that owned my mom found out she was expecting puppies, he was going to do away with us! Gratefully, a visiting neighbor would not allow it. She borrowed my mom, promising to return her once we were born, and vowed to find homes for all of us pups.

I met the Farm Lady when I was just a few days old. Although she has four children, it was the oldest daughter that came with her to visit me weekly. They cuddled all the puppies, which was a lot because there were nine of us! The Farm Lady got the first choice of the litter and she picked me! She said, "That one! We like the sweet one with the big white heart shape on her head." I couldn't wait for the day that I could go home with the Farm Lady and meet the whole family!

When I arrived at her farm, the Farm Lady put a red bandana around my neck, which made me feel like an important part of the family. But there was a big and wonderful surprise waiting for me at the farm: his name was Chase, and he was a full grown border collie that looked very much like me, only bigger. I was so excited to see him that I jumped all over him showering him with kisses and being a real pest. "Let's play! Let's play!" I would beg. Though he was very patient, he finally had enough and let out a gentle but firm growl. We have been the best of friends since. It was Chase who taught me how to act on the farm.

For the first few weeks, the Farm Lady had me sleep in a crate by her bed, and I was slowly introduced to the outdoors. I couldn't wait to have a job like Chase's and get working! As the spring turned to summer, I spent more and more time working outdoors on the farm. Eventually, I became Chase's full-time companion outside.

Chase and I were always busy, busy! Each morning, while the Farm Lady fed the farm animals, we would run along the fence lines, chasing goats, llamas, and anything that would run from us. Back and forth we would go, nipping to get the pasture animals to move. It was great fun! Chase told me: "This is how I got my name; I love to chase things. I used to leave the property and chase things but that was dangerous and it scares the Farm Lady. Always stay on the farm. There are plenty of things to chase here." Chase taught me how to protect the farm animals too, because they belong to the Farm Lady.

As I grew from pup to young dog, I became very athletic and began to be known for the amazing things I could do! My most impressive feat is that I can stand with all four paws on top of the fence rail. I can jump any fence and escape any kennel. I never tire either. Even after a long run with the Farm Lady, I come home and get right back to work.

I love all my jobs, but my favorite is patrolling the bunny farm. On sunny days, the Farm Lady lets the bunnies out of their hutches to run around a fenced area. I love to crouch low and see how close I can get to them. Although I could jump over the fence from a standstill if I wanted to, I never do. I would never hurt her bunnies.

I am a kissy dog and I will even jump straight up and plant a kiss on someone's face! I love all people, especially kids, like the Farm Lady's daughter, her other children and their friends. I also love belly rubs- so much that I will run up to humans I don't even know and flip upside down so they can give me a belly scratch. I know a few other tricks too, like "shake" and "play dead" and "get sneaky" where I crawl low on the ground. I love to do these tricks because people always laugh and clap.

The Farm Lady was so impressed with my speed and athletic skills that she enrolled us in dog agility school. Each Saturday morning we went to a class where I ran through tunnels and over bridges and ramps, weaved through poles, and jumped bars. I couldn't get enough of it! I was so good at it that my teacher called me "Little Miss Perfect." What I liked most about agility school was being with the Farm Lady. I love the Farm Lady and she really loves me.

That's why what happened next made me so sad and confused. One day a sign went up on the farm: For Sale. The Farm Lady explained to me; "Bella, with the kids getting older and beginning to move out, we feel that a smaller place might be better for us." Then a big truck came and took all the family's chairs and boxes and we all moved to a smaller home on the lake. At first, it was fun exploring the new place. I looked for rodents and frogs in the marshes and enjoyed drinking from the water and chasing the waves. But there was something very sad in me. I missed the farm and I missed my jobs. There were no goats to herd and no bunnies to protect and the yard was so small, I could hardly run around.

And then one day I found myself in a bit of trouble. I didn't mean to leave the yard, but I was running and the yard is so small… and the next thing I knew I was off on a field trip away from the Farm Lady. I was enjoying exploring my new surroundings but I knew the Farm Lady would be looking for me and my tummy reminded me it was time for dinner, so I began to head back. As I turned around, a big yellow dog blocked my way. I could tell she was trouble as she showed me her teeth and I felt threatened. Soon a scary gray dog joined her and they began growling at me. I tried to get them to run off by nipping at their feet like I did with the llamas but they thought I wanted to fight! As they both started to approach me, I got so scared that I bit the scary gray dog and ran for my life!

I could hear the dogs chasing me but I am "Little Miss Perfect" in agility class so I ran faster! I jumped over a fence, tunneled through an old log, ran across a fallen tree, weaved through the bushes and soon the dogs gave up and went back. As I got back home, I remembered how Chase had told me to never leave the yard. The Farm Lady looked worried and she knew somehow that I had been in some trouble and that I was not adjusting well to the lake. I thought the whole thing was over, but the next day the dogs found out where I lived and paid me a visit. Chase ignored them as they stood at the yard's edge and growled at us. I tried to ignore them too, but as the yellow dog moved into MY yard, I darted after her and nipped her tail. That was the end of the lake life for me.

That evening, the lady packed up all my things and drove me back to the farm. I thought it was going to be a happy event, but it didn't take me long to realize I was there, all alone. There were no bunnies to protect, no Chase to play with, and no family to snuggle up with at night. The Farm Lady visited me several times a day and she would say, "Soon Bella, we will find you a new farm to live on and a new farm family to love. Don't worry." But I was VERY worried. I wanted this farm, and this loving family, and Chase and my job! I wanted everything back just the way it was! I wanted to tag along with the Farm Man when he mows the lawn and get belly rubs from the Farm Lady's daughter and show off my tricks to the farm guests!

A week or so later, the Farm Lady and Farm Man came to the farm for what I thought was just a visit, but they looked sad. As the Farm Man packed up my bowl and my leash and my special blanket, the Farm Lady said, "Beautiful Bella, we found a loving family on a small farm nearby. You will love it there. I will visit you often…" Her voice trailed off as tears filled her eyes. She told the Farm Man that she was too upset to take me there, so he agreed and loaded my things in the back of the truck and he and I jumped in the cab. As the Farm Man and I drove off, I looked out the back window at the Farm Lady. As she waved with tears in her eyes, I sank into the seat and tried to hide.

The new farm was much smaller. They had a few chickens, but no bunnies and no goats and no llamas. They had two donkeys but I was told not to mess with them. The farm family had a daughter, much younger than the Farm Lady's daughter, but very nice. She seemed to take a liking to me, but I just wanted to go home. She took off my bandana and put on a blue collar, which made me even more unhappy because my bandana meant so much to me. The blue collar had a special button on it that would beep if I left the fence-lined farm. The Farm Man looked very sad as he unpacked my things.

As the Farm Man chatted with the man of the small farm, I could tell there was some kind of problem. Apparently, there was some electrical issue with the fence and the collar was not working. The two men tried hard to fix it but couldn't. They were afraid that I would run off and that would be dangerous for me so they decided that until the fence was fixed, I should go back to my old farm. I couldn't get out of there fast enough! As the Farm Man packed up my things, I grabbed my bandana with my teeth and jumped back into the cab of the truck. You should have seen the sheer joy and delight on the Farm Lady's face as the Farm Man came back with me! I was standing proud and happy in the front seat!

The next week at the farm was one of the best. The Farm Lady and Farm Man spent more and more time on the farm. The Lady and I practiced agility, jumping and running through tunnels and I followed the Farm Man as he mowed the lawn, stopping occasionally to throw me a ball. The Farm Man and Farm Lady laughed so hard as they saw me sitting on the fence! The Farm family seemed so happy back visiting the farm and it was so quiet and peaceful there. The Farm Lady even stayed late and we spent the evening on our favorite bench, looking at the stars. I knew, however, it was just a matter of time until the small farm fence would be fixed and I would leave this life forever.

Then one day, I waited and waited, but the Farm Lady didn't come all day. I began to worry. It wasn't until almost evening that I heard a big truck rumbling up the road and into the driveway. I was afraid it was the family coming to take me to the small farm so I hid in the very back of my doghouse. When I heard the truck doors slam, I peeked out to get a look and spotted a huge truck, just like the one that took all the family's boxes and chairs and things from the farm to the lake. I crept back in my house, staying very small and quiet so I could not be seen.

Then I heard voices. It was the Farm Lady calling my name! "Bella! Belly Girl! We're Home!" Home? I couldn't believe my big Belly ears!! I bounced out of my hiding place and ran to her, jumped up and planted a big Belly kiss on the Farm Lady's face. Everyone was there, even Chase. As the Farm Man took down the For Sale sign and the family unloaded their boxes, the Farm Lady and I snuggled up on our favorite bench and looked up at the stars. She said rubbing my belly, "You knew all along, didn't you Bella? You are a farm dog and we are a farm family. We belong on this farm together." I could not have agreed more.

The next morning, Chase and I got up early and went straight to work!

The real Bella

The real Chase

69272917R00029

Made in the USA
San Bernardino, CA
13 February 2018